American Pride

COMPILED BY JILL LIBERMAN

emmis

books

CINCINNATI, OHIO

AMERICAN PRIDE
Famous Americans Celebrate the USA

ISBN 1-57860-150-9

Photography credits:
BARRY BONDS / Photo by Steve Hathaway Photography
JANN CARL / Photo by Ron Derhacopian
LEE GREENWOOD / Photo courtesy of Curb Records
PRIEST HOLMES / Photo by Hank Young
THE AMAZING KRESKIN / Photo by Ray Ferry
MARIE OSMOND / Photo by Art Streiber/Icon International
BOBBY RIVERS / Photo by Joseph Sinnott/WNET New York
DANIEL RODRIGUEZ / Photo by Michael Halsband
3 DOORS DOWN / Photo by Phin Daly
JEAN-CLAUDE VAN DAMME / Photo by Michael McCreary/Haven Studio
MONTEL WILLIAMS / Photo courtesy of Paramount Pictures Corporation
PAULA ZAHN / Photo courtesy of Andrew Eccles/CNN

Jacket and interior:
Stephen Sullivan

ABOUT JILL LIBERMAN

Jill is a television producer and former radio talk show host. She lives in Boca Raton, Florida, with her husband and son.

American Pride is Ms. Liberman's first book.

Please direct inquiries and comments regarding *American Pride* to info@americanpride.com

THIS BOOK IS DEDICATED TO the men and women who put their lives on the line to honor and protect our country; the sons, daughters, and parents who forego the comforts of home to preserve our freedom; those who confront danger to keep us safe ... those who selflessly sacrifice to defend America; the families that have endured lonely nights and perilous times; my grandfather, father, friends, family, and all who have answered this nation's call ... YOU ARE AMERICAN PRIDE.

I salute you.

Jill Liberman

ACKNOWLEDGMENTS

Adam and Stan—you are my heart. Thank you for your help, support, and patience ★ Elese and Dan Itzler for instilling in me that anything is possible ★ Richard Hunt and Jack Heffron for believing in this book from the start ★ Steve Sullivan for his follow-up and patience ★ Howard Cohen for spreading the word ★ Jon Greene for his support and guidance ★ Jesse for sharing the "crazy" gene ★ Each and every participant who contributed and showed American Pride ★ The agents, managers, publicists, and personal assistants who came through for me ★ Dulcie and Wally Shanbron for their interest and enthusiasm ★ Steven Weiner for his help ★ My siblings for being who they are ★ You, the readers, for helping me accomplish my goal of spreading American pride and spirit ★

MEMBERS AND FAMILY MEMBERS OF THE MILITARY ARE SUBJECT TO UNIQUE STRESS DUE TO THE NATURE OF MILITARY LIFE. A PERCENTAGE OF THE SALES OF *AMERICAN PRIDE* WILL BE DONATED TO TWO ORGANIZATIONS DEDICATED TO HELPING IN TIMES OF NEED THE FAMILIES OF MEN AND WOMEN IN THE MILITARY SERVICE. I AM HONORED TO BE ASSOCIATED WITH THEM THROUGH THIS PROJECT.

The Air Force Aid Society (AFAS) is the official charity of The U.S. Air Force, and was incorporated in 1942. It is a non-profit organization whose mission is to relieve financial distress of Air Force members and their families and to assist them in financing their higher education goals. EVERY DOLLAR DONATED goes directly to their emergency assistance programs. The AFAS helped over 34,000 families last year. The AFAS provides emergency assistance to members of the Air Force and their families, sponsors educational assistance programs, and offers community enhancement programs that improve member welfare. Visit the web site at www.afas.org.

Army Emergency Relief (AER) is a non-profit organization incorporated in 1942 by the Secretary of War and the Army Chief of Staff. AER's sole mission is to help soldiers and their dependents. AER is the Army's own emergency financial assistance organization and is dedicated to "Helping the Army Take Care of Its Own." Among those the AER helps are soldiers on extended active duty and their dependents, and widow(ers) and orphans of soldiers who died while on active duty or after they retired. The AER has helped more than 2.8 million soldiers and their families overcome financial emergencies over the last sixty years. AER helps provide emergency financial needs for food, rent, utilities, and funeral expenses. The AER provides financial scholarships based on financial need to children of soldiers. Visit the web site at www.aerhq.org.

INTRODUCTION

One morning I woke up with an idea for a coffee-table book. The concept was to have celebrities, athletes, politicians, and prominent businesspeople join together in a book to share their thoughts on what living in America means to them. The idea really excited me. Americans are fascinated with celebrity, and what a powerful way, I thought, to help promote American pride and spirit. The tragic events of September 11, the war, and all the challenges our country faces right now had left me with a personal need to honor and pay tribute to America. I wanted to give something back to my country as a way of expressing my American pride. Until that moment, I didn't know how or what.

I am not a writer. I am a television producer who took time off from work to be a mom. Most of my time is spent carpooling, not calling celebrities. The only thing I've written is a grocery list. The thought of putting together a book and trying to publish it was a bit daunting, but I felt I had to try.

I began by compiling a list of potential participants as if I were planning a party, keeping the list varied and interesting. My son helped me with the names of athletes and celebrities that appeal to his generation, and my husband happily added his contributions to the list. In fact, as I began mentioning the book to people, it seemed that everyone I knew had a suggestion on who would be a good participant. Wherever I went, my list became the entertainment. I would hand out paper and a pen and take suggestions. My nieces and nephews predictably named pop stars, in the hope that by having their favorite performers participate in the book somehow they would get to meet them. My father went the more intellectual route of Supreme Court Justices. My cousin Robbin, an avid reader, contributed names of authors and journalists to the mix. In no time I had a long and eclectic list. It was time to put the plan into action. The next step was to compile a list of contact numbers for each participant. This would have been easy if I had a phone book filled with phone numbers of celebrities. I didn't. I went down the list and tackled each name one by one. I called anyone associated with that person. For example, to contact soap opera stars, I might begin by calling the network on which their show appears.

Many times it took A LOT of calls just to reach the right person, and there were a few people whom I didn't reach. There were other instances when I needed to go through several representatives to get an answer. I now know what is meant by "my people"—as in, "have your people call my people." There are agents, managers, publicists, attorneys, personal assistants, and PR firms, all of whom want to be in the loop. Working through so many layers meant finding additional numbers and trying to determine the ultimate contact person.

Once I lined up enough contact numbers, it was time to put them to use. I began calling people to invite them to participate in the book. On the first day of calling, I got commitments from two celebrities—Jackie Mason and Raoul Felder. FedEx packages arrived the next day with their photos and quotes. The book was taking shape. Most of the people I spoke with were very enthusiastic, although I did speak with one agent who was quick to point out that his clients "don't do books." I feel that this particular agent did a disservice to his clients by never even presenting the offer to them. More than once an agent "passed" on behalf of his clients without ever offering it to or discussing it with them. Those agents, however, were few and far between. A large part of my joy and satisfaction from compiling the book came from learning that the contributors share my passion and patriotism for this country. I didn't know what to expect in terms of the contributions I would receive. It proved both rewarding and refreshing to know that all the people who participated in the book were eager to share their thoughts on living in America and were happy to contribute to the project. To my surprise, several of the book's contributors even made the time to contact me personally to thank me for including them and for compiling such a worthwhile book.

I came up with the title *American Pride* at the same time I thought of the idea for the book. From what I understand, books can change titles as often as people change socks, but this title stuck. I wanted to donate a portion of my profit from the sales of the book to charity. I researched patriotic charities and selected the Army Emergency Relief Fund and the Air Force Aid Society, both of which benefit families of the U.S. Military. It is truly my wish that through *American Pride* I can make a difference and help these families of the men and women in our military who make the ultimate sacrifice to help keep America safe and free. One of the most fulfilling moments of the book, for me, was contacting the charities and letting them know a check was on its way!

I gave myself four weeks of serious, focused attention to put the project together. I often spent more than fifteen hours per day working on it, trying to balance the ideals of the book with the practical necessities of family life. My goal was to have over 50 contributors. At the end of the four weeks, that goal had been achieved. Though I was proud to have reached my goal, I was sad to see the project end. I didn't realize that, in some ways, it was just beginning. Because this is my first book, I was unfamiliar with how the publishing world works. As luck would have it, my husband's cousin Steve knew somebody who knew somebody who had published a book. I spoke to the publisher, and the rest, as they say, is history.

When I thought of compiling *American Pride*, it immediately felt right. I never stopped to think about how I would reach such high-profile people. It also never even occurred to me that people might decline to participate. Who wouldn't want to show pride in America? I was genuinely taken aback when I received my first "no." So much so that I outwardly expressed my surprise. Too busy? How could someone be too busy to submit a few sentences? Five minutes after we hung up the phone, I received a call from that person saying he'd had a change of heart and of course he would participate! The passion I have for this project is unsurpassed by any other project in which I have ever been involved. I can't put in words the emotions I felt and the determination I was able to muster to make this book a reality. I admit there were times when I wondered if I would succeed. People wouldn't hesitate to tell me stories of how difficult it is to get published. When I felt I had come so far, I was told by a "friend" I had a long way to go. But mostly I wore blinders. I compared myself to an athlete training for a marathon. No matter how tired I was from "working out," I knew I could push myself just a little more. And I did. Never did working on this book feel like work. Compiling *American Pride* was very much a labor of love. I enjoyed every moment of it. It was a thrill for me to read each submission as it arrived, and I would marvel at what people wrote. I couldn't wait to call my parents, friends, and anyone who would listen as I enthusiastically shared the newest participant's thoughts on living in America. The agents, assistants, and publicists I worked with were an absolute pleasure. As for the book's participants, I couldn't be happier with everyone who chose to share his or her thoughts. If I were planning a party, they would all be on my list. I'll miss coming to work every day. Funny, people are STILL offering names for additional contributors. Maybe it's time to start Volume Two!

CONTRIBUTORS ★ ★ ★ ★ ★ ★ ★ ★ ★ ★ ★ ★

Christina Applegate-Schaech & John Schaech

Jeff Bagwell

U.S. Senator Evan Bayh

Justin Berfield

Lance Berkman

Corbin Bernsen

Barry Bonds

David Brenner

Morgan Brittany

Aaron Brooks

Dr. Joyce Brothers

Bobbi Brown

Judge Joe Brown

President George W. Bush

Jann Carl

Dixie Carter

Harry Wayne Casey

Susie Castillo

David Copperfield

Mark Cuban

Michael Dell

Phyllis Diller

Jack Dreyfus

Herman Edwards

Erik Estrada

Chris Evert

Doug E. Fresh

Josh Gracin

Lee Greenwood

Mia Hamm

Frederick O. Hanser

Lynn Herring

Priest Holmes

H. Wayne Huizenga

Peter Jennings

Sean Kanan

★ ★ ★ ★ ★ ★ ★ ★ ★ ★ ★ ★ ★ ★ ★ ★

Don King

The Amazing Kreskin

Cheryl Ladd & Brian Russell

U.S. Senator Frank R. Lautenberg

Tommy Lee

Carl Lindner

Peyton Manning

Jackie Mason & Raoul Felder

Deuce McAllister

Darryl "DMC" McDaniels

Dennis Miller

Randy Moss

Marie Osmond

Paula Jai Parker

Alex Penelas

Chad Pennington

Ross Perot

Lou Piniella

Peerless Price

Bobby Rivers

Anthony Robbins

Daniel Rodriguez

Christy Carlson Romano

Pat Sajak

Arnold Schwarzenegger

Jeff Smulyan

Jerry Springer

Bill Stoneman

Isiah Thomas

Richard Thomas

3 Doors Down

Donald Trump

Jean-Claude Van Damme

Montel Williams

Paula Zahn

Jacklyn Zeman

At Game 7 of the World Series … the American flag was blowing freely out in the outfield. "The Star-Spangled Banner" was coming to a close with the lyrics "the land of the free and the home of the brave … " the Air Force jets roared overhead.

I turned to my wife with tears in my eyes and said, "We are so lucky to be born in this country." She said, "Yes we are, but honey … there's no crying in baseball."

CHRISTINA APPLEGATE-SCHAECH & JOHN SCHAECH
Actors

It's truly overwhelming, what it's like to be an American. **It's beyond the realm of words.** To look at all the fans—who wear red, white, and blue and wave American flags at the stadiums all over the U.S.A.—gives you great pride. This has been an incredible time for our country. I am so proud and honored to live and work in America. The recent times have been a great awakening for all of us and have truly put life in perspective. With two young daughters, I want them to understand how important it is to honor our country and the opportunities they will have that so many other children around the world will not.

JEFF BAGWELL
First baseman, Houston Astros

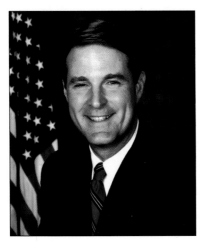

My first job after school was working for a district court judge in the Southern District of Indiana. I learned a lot about the judiciary, and I learned a lot about life watching what took place in that courtroom. One of the highlights every year was the ceremony where we inducted new citizens into our country. And for those of you who haven't had the opportunity to see one of these events, I encourage you to do it. It's one of the great, truly great, American scenes. It'll make you proud of our country. People would come into the courtroom—every size, shape, description, nationality. They'd dress in their finest clothes. They'd be surrounded by their family members and their closest friends. They'd be clutching a little flag that the court had given them. And the look of pride upon their faces, at the prospect of joining us in this country, is something that's very hard to describe. At the appointed hour the judge would come in, and he'd ask everyone to rise, to raise their right hand, and to swear an oath of allegiance—an oath of allegiance not to any race, or any ethnic group, or any political party, but **an oath of allegiance to an idea. It's an idea that we call America.**

For more than two hundred years our national experience has been a journey in pursuit of that idea. A restless, dynamic journey, seeking more hope and opportunity and freedom for every American—the people in that courtroom and now what has grown to be more than 260 million of our fellow citizens. We've traveled a long way. We've come far. There's been so much change during this time. We broke the bonds of slavery. We enfranchised women. We triumphed over the Great Depression and the twin tyrannies of communism and fascism. But throughout all the change, and down through all the years, what is right, what is true, what is essential about our nation, our core values and principles have remained very much the same.

EVAN BAYH
U.S. Senator, Indiana

To be a kid growing up in America
has presented me with not only a
chance to entertain but to have a life
full of happiness and opportunity.

JUSTIN BERFIELD
Actor and Ronald McDonald House Youth Ambassador

It's a great blessing to be in a country that allows us such freedoms. I celebrate the opportunity to be in this wonderful democracy each day. We live in a country where we can pursue our dreams and exchange ideas.

As a baseball player, I have to admit that what we do pales in comparison to the great sacrifices from our troops. I can't begin to thank them and honor them enough for what they do. On behalf of our entire team and my family, we salute the men and women who have bravely fought for our right to freedom.

LANCE BERKMAN
Outfielder, Houston Astros

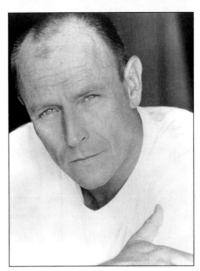

My father's side of the family comes from Germany, Russia, and various European countries over many decades. A portion of my mother's lineage is Scottish, but there's also a good dose of Cherokee in there. With that in mind, I visualize the landscape around me, "my America," to be a place where sanctuary and liberty are provided for all. It is a land of opportunity and responsibility for all its people, whatever their lineage. It is the last bit of pioneered earth created by stock from all corners of the globe, and to that end it must represent what we as inhabitants of this planet want whatever and whoever else is out there to believe we are. This is not a burden but an honor. This is not an invitation but an expectation. This is living life to its greatest capacity. This is living in America.

CORBIN BERNSEN
Actor

When I hear the national anthem played before every game, I still get goose bumps. I am consistently reminded of how proud I am to be an American. We live in a country where the the freedoms we value so highly allow us to reach for the stars and see our dreams come true. I am extremely grateful to our fellow countrymen and women who have fought for our country, sacrificing their lives for our freedom.

As Americans, we must remember that our **freedom does not come without a price.** We must support our troops, our government, and most important, our president, regardless of our political views, in these times of uncertainty.

Being an American doesn't necessarily mean you were born on U.S. soil. It means that no matter what race, religion, or background you came from, you can take advantage of the opportunities this country offers and live out the American Dream.

BARRY BONDS
Outfielder, San Francisco Giants

DAVID BRENNER
Comedian, author of I Think There's a Terrorist in My Soup

To me, living in America is having the rare opportunity that upon awakening the next morning and every morning thereafter, we have the freedom and the means to **make it a better day than yesterday for ourselves and for our fellow man.** For in this land, hope springs eternal, and dreams can be forever realized.

We have the right, actually the obligation, to do battle with anyone and everyone who threatens to usurp or destroy this, whether they are from outside or from within our borders, whether they are a foreign government or our own government.

We have the obligation to pass down to our children for them to protect and pass down to their children this special gift we call the American Dream.

To think, some young man
or woman whom I have never
met and probably never will,
is willing to put their life on the
line to preserve MY freedom.

THAT is America!

MORGAN BRITTANY
Actor

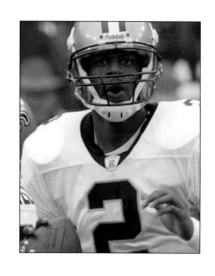

The reason I am proud to live and play in America is because this is the only place in the world where you can enjoy freedom on and off the field, thanks to the patriotism of today's American soldiers.

AARON BROOKS
Quarterback, New Orleans Saints

A wonderful thing about America is that opportunity is available to all Americans no matter what your station in life, what your national origin, race, religion, or disabilities. While not all barriers to advancement have been completely eradicated, this country has led the world in lowering impediments to advancement. It continues to ascribe to equal treatment  for everyone. In America you are not born into a caste or class system that you are consigned to for the rest of your life. You can advance as far as your ability, hard work, and discipline can take you. Examples abound of people who have reached the highest levels in every field strictly on their own abilities. It is not perfect by any means, but we believe as Americans that we can make it better in all fields—politics, arts, science, finance, government, education, and every other field imaginable. Opportunity abounds, and that is the greatest attraction for people all over the world who want to become Americans.

DR. JOYCE BROTHERS
Psychologist and syndicated columnist

BOBBI BROWN
CEO, Bobbi Brown Cosmetics

America is a place where you have the freedom to use your knowledge and

creativity to make
something out of nothing.

Living in America means that I am at the nexus of world events, all races and cultures, and at the center of the world's future. America is a place where, for better or worse, the problems of mankind will be worked out. Our country is both a challenge and a promise, a place to be a hero and truly one of the brave, and it is a place of struggle. It is all of these things so that it will eventually be the land of the free. To be in on all of this is a great thing.

JOE BROWN
Television personality and former district court judge

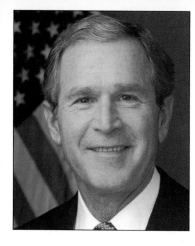

GEORGE W. BUSH
President of the United States of America

We count our blessings, and there are many to count.

We are thankful for the families that share our life in this land of liberty.
We are thankful for the opportunities given to us every day in this country.
And we are thankful for our freedom, and the freedom declared by our
Founding Fathers, defended by so many generations and granted to each one
of us by Almighty God.

Americans know that our country did not come about by chance. Our nation was first designed as a colony, serving an empire and answering to a king. The Founders had other things in mind. In the summer of 1776, they declared that these colonies are and of right ought to be free and independent states. Americans can draw a straight line from the free lives we live today to that one moment when the world changed forever.

From that day in 1776, freedom has had a home and a defender. Unlike any other country, America came into the world with a message for mankind, that all are created equal and are meant to be free.

There is no American race, there is only an American creed. We believe in the dignity and rights of every person. We believe in equal justice, limited government and the rule of law, personal responsibility, and tolerance toward others. This creed of freedom and equality has lifted the lives of millions of Americans, of citizens by birth and citizens by choice. This creed draws our friends to us, sets our enemies against us, and always inspires the best that is in us.

We have seen that American patriotism is still a living faith. We love our country only more when she is threatened. America is the most diverse nation on earth, yet in a moment we discovered again that we are a single people. We share the same allegiance, we live under the same flag—and when you strike one American, you strike us all.

More than ever in the lifetimes of most Americans, our flag stands for a true, united country. We've been united in our grief, and we are united in our resolve to protect people and defeat the enemies of freedom.

Many of you have family members serving in the military—wherever they are stationed, this nation is depending on them, and you can be proud of them.

America's servicemen and servicewomen and our veterans know better than anyone that our love for our country is shown in works. That spirit is alive and strong in America today. As we fight a war abroad at home, Americans are answering the call of service, giving their time and energy to causes greater than self-interest. This nation is confronting a terrible evil with good.

Today, as much as ever before, America bears the hopes of the world.

Yet, from the day of founding, America's own great hope has never been in ourselves alone. The Founders humbly sought the wisdom and the blessing of Divine Providence. May we always live by that same trust, and may God continue to watch over the United States of America.

Ron Derhacopian

My great-great-grandfather came to the United States in the early 1840's. Since he was very poor, he had no way to pay for his passage. A farmer in Missouri agreed to pay for his journey. In return, Grandpa Carl became an indentured servant, which meant three years of farm labor for no pay. He gladly gave up these precious years so that he could be free and have the chance to follow his dreams. He left his family, and everything he knew, so that future generations could live in this land of opportunity. I am grateful for his vision and sacrifice.

But I am also grateful to *all* the Americans who have made this country what it is today—to the Founding Fathers who laid the foundation for our freedoms; to the men and women of our armed forces who have protected these freedoms with the greatest sacrifice of all; to the settlers who forged westward and built a country; to the Americans filled with ingenuity who created everything from the flight of man to the computer. And to all in between who raise their families, go to work, and volunteer their time. By living the American dream, we all help keep it alive.

I am thankful my children were born in this amazing country. I am filled with hope that their dreams will come true, as mine have. And I hope that they will do their part to keep America strong and free.

God Bless America.

JANN CARL
Host, "Entertainment Tonight"

The United States of America is a great sprawling family of individuals, who agree on some things and disagree on other things, always remembering that we are one: one family, bound by a covenant drawn from the supreme effort of individuals who also agreed and disagreed, and lived and died together for their dream of freedom and hope.

At our best, we Americans accept that we are children of destiny, and accept love of country as primal.

At our best, we Americans make strength out of difference; we argue vociferously and change peacefully.

At our best, we Americans remember that we are one and indivisible, that we have inherited hope, and that we must pass it on.

DIXIE CARTER
Actor

I love living in America because it allows me to be who I am, what I am, and what I want to be. It allows me to dream and allows for my dreams to come true. Living in America, I can enjoy the freedom and choices that other countries forbid.

HARRY WAYNE CASEY
Musician, KC and the Sunshine Band

To me, being an American means that I can wake up in the morning knowing that I can get out of life what I put into it. I know that my dreams can come true through hard work and dedication and that I can achieve amazing heights. I have the freedom to do as I choose! Being well aware of how human beings, especially women, are treated in other countries, it makes me especially proud to say that I live in the United States of America, the land of the free.

SUSIE CASTILLO
Miss U.S.A.® 2003

As an illusionist, my life and work are devoted to proving that **nothing is impossible. America is the supreme embodiment of that idea.**

Like parents pass DNA to their children, the Founding Fathers passed along a spark of their spirit to all of us fortunate enough to be Americans. It's a spirit composed of 18-karat courage, vision, thinking out of the box, and never taking no for an answer.

America is the only country in the world where a middle-class kid from New Jersey can make a career for himself by doing magic, no less. In America the ceiling has been removed, you can grow as much as you want, you have the freedom to create the life you want for yourself and others. For me, America is about the highest and best use of freedom. It's about having an idea, believing in it, and making it come true.

Being an American is the greatest gift I could ask for.

DAVID COPPERFIELD
Illusionist

Living in America means every morning when you wake up you have the opportunity to make your dreams come true.

If it can happen to me, it can happen to anyone.

MARK CUBAN
Owner, Dallas Mavericks

As a young boy in Houston, I dreamed of one day having a business with an American flag flying out front. To me, that image symbolized opportunity, accomplishment, community, and pride. Since then, I've been fortunate to realize that dream in many locations around the world.

Of course, in most of those places, the flag of another country flies next to the American flag. And I've come to understand how that scene represents an even more complete vision of the values I've held so deeply for so many years. America is more than a place or a people. America is a spirit, embraced by anyone who follows their dreams – regardless what flag is flying out front.

MICHAEL DELL
Chairman & CEO, Dell

All you have to do to realize you live in the world's greatest country is travel.

Every time you come back to the U.S.A., you know that no matter how

we stumble along with ongoing problems, our country is the greatest,

based on the best ideas of some dear old men.

PHYLLIS DILLER
Actor, author and painter

 If my mother were still alive, one thing she would tell you is for her son to have become one of the wealthiest men in the United States is impossible—if there were a stronger word, she would use it. Last she knew, I had three different jobs, at fifteen dollars a week, and hadn't made a go of any of them. It was no secret to my family that I would have a hard time making a living. My mother would call me a nice boy, but lazy, with no ambition at all. What a country!

JACK DREYFUS
Founder, The Dreyfus Fund

American pride. It means the freedom to pursue your dreams and strive to be your best. It means that we care for and defend the freedoms that our forefathers fought so valiantly for. Above all else, American pride is about embracing a nation of people who represent different cultures, different beliefs, and varying backgrounds and working together to better the lives of all Americans.

HERMAN EDWARDS
Head Coach, New York Jets

Growing up in the projects of Spanish Harlem, New York City, I remember the different neighborhood groups based on heritage: Puerto Rican, Italian, Irish, etc. But the one thing we all had in common was that we were Americans. As a Latino child from the projects, my mother always said her dream was that her children would get an education, work hard, and prosper in life. Her dream came true.

I had a dream to become an actor, and it became a reality. Now my children have dreams of their own; and God willing, theirs will come to fruition too. All because we, as Americans, have been blessed to live in a country where we have the freedom to dream, to live, to hope, and to strive to make our dreams come true. Mine have, and each time I see that glorious flag, I count my blessings and remember why I am so very proud and honored to be an American. God bless America now and forever.

ERIK ESTRADA
Actor

I am very fortunate to have been born in America—the greatest country in the world! This country has afforded me the freedom to pursue a career in the sport that I love. The opportunity to enjoy a career in tennis is one that women in many other countries aren't given. America offers all who live here unlimited opportunity as long as we live within our democratic laws.

We are a giving country. We have compassion for the less fortunate in our country, and we also give unselfishly to other nations.

I am privileged to have traveled the world, but always enjoy returning home to this country. I love the U.S.A.

CHRIS EVERT
Tennis champion

I love living in America because

America is the only country where you can relate to so many different kinds of people, all with a common cause of freedom.

DOUG E. FRESH
Hip-hop entertainer

I love living in America because of the freedom of choice my family and I have and the pride our country gives me with the sense of knowing that any opportunities available are achievable, not only for myself, but for my family. It also enables me to prove to my children that anything can be achieved if they work hard enough and make it their personal goals to achieve them.

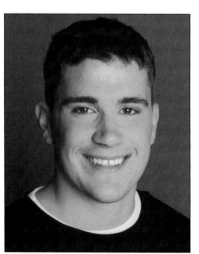

JOSH GRACIN
*Lance Corporal, United States Marine Corps and
"American Idol" finalist*

I'm sometimes overwhelmed by this vast nation and wish I could see how America will change in the next one hundred years. As long as we continue to dream, create inventions, and solve the challenges of an ever-expanding population, we will have the power to create a better society. But it is inevitable that the freedom, liberty, and can-do attitude that characterize us will be challenged, sometimes in ways that leave us no choice but to defend ourselves and the land that we love. It happened in 1941 at Pearl Harbor and again in 2001 at the World Trade Center and the Pentagon.

I wrote "God Bless the U.S.A." in 1983 to bring people together. We have our differences, and that is one of the many strengths of our country. But even if we don't agree on economics or politics, I hope this song can let us sing together as Americans and perhaps our differences won't matter so much.

I pray that God, who has watched over this nation for more than two hundred years, will not forsake us. And I pray that God would keep us safe from those who would do us harm. I pray for America, " 'cause there ain't no doubt I love this land. God Bless the U.S.A."

LEE GREENWOOD
Singer/songwriter

I have played in numerous countries throughout my career, and my favorite place to play is America. Our fans give us unconditional support and always appreciate the value of hard work and determination. It is an honor to represent the Red, White, and Blue each time we take the field.

MIA HAMM
U.S. Olympic and
World Cup Soccer champion

"**Lucky**" is the first word that comes to mind, to be born into the greatest country in the history of the world. Our freedom, independence, and prosperity are symbols of hope for so many around the world who have immigrated or otherwise still strive to become a part of this great experiment. But all of us must remember our obligation to be vigilant and proactive in protecting these basic rights and in encouraging them around the world as it grows smaller and smaller. I feel fortunate to be a part of the great game of baseball, which is so central to the culture and fabric of America. Baseball in many ways is a symbol of the great American Dream.

FREDERICK O. HANSER
Owner & Vice Chairman, St. Louis Cardinals

America means the joy of watching my two sons grow up knowing they can be whatever they wish...all the endless possibilities. They can make their own dreams come true, as I did mine.

LYNN HERRING
Actor

It is great to be an American when you are a young man and you see men fifty and older volunteering to fight the war on terror.

It makes you understand and believe that you should **never give up** on any endeavor in life.

PRIEST HOLMES
Running Back, Kansas City Chiefs

Hank Young

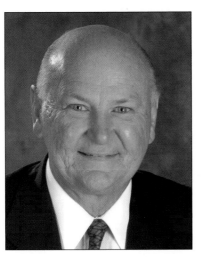

The concept of freedom summarizes my feelings about being an American. The fact that we are truly a free people punctuates every minute of American life. Freedom of speech, freedom of activity, freedom of movement. I like the words from a song, or maybe it was a book: "You are free to be you, and I am free to be me."

H. WAYNE HUIZENGA
Chairman, Huizenga Holdings, Inc.

One of the beauties of living in America is that the American story is a journey in itself.

Two hundred and sixteen years after the Constitution, we are reminded every day that we are living the Founding Fathers' ideas, and ideals, and contradictions. They created a remarkable document, which they intended to be handed down, like a precious family heirloom, and reinterpreted when needed from generation to generation.

Living in America for all these years, I know that America's principles have been molded, adapted, shaken, and assaulted, but remarkably they endure.

PETER JENNINGS
Anchor, ABC News

The steel of our nation has been tempered in the forge of adversity. We are still a young nation, imperfect. Yet we continue to grow and learn. It is our diversity that strengthens us and provides the opportunity for every man, woman, and child to pursue their dreams and fulfill their potential. This freedom shines as a beacon to the rest of the world, illuminating what is possible.

SEAN KANAN
Actor/writer/producer

I love America! Our Founding Fathers, in their infinite wisdom, had a dream of a land of Freedom, Liberty, Equality, and Justice for All and created a fundamental document called the Constitution with its Bill of Rights. I take great pride in being an American who is a beneficiary of the reality of this dream.

Through prayer, faith, imagination, innovation, and perseverance, we make our constitutional document a living reality where every person of every color, nationality, and religion alike can realize his or her dream.

America is a promise of opportunity. Where else but in America can a minority, an African-American like me, survive and succeed in spite of the many inequities and injustices that we have endured? As Martin Luther King so eloquently said, "Injustice anywhere is a threat to justice everywhere.... We shall overcome." As long as we believe in the principles upon which this great nation was founded, we shall overcome—working together, for a better America.

This is the greatest nation in the world.

Only in America!

DON KING
Boxing promoter, President & CEO, Don King Productions

As I have traveled during my career some 3 million miles, I've been haunted by a thought… that I could have been born some other place outside the U.S.A., from where I would look upon America with envious yearning and frustration that I was not growing up in such a richly rewarding land.

No wonder we are envied. What country has sacrificed so many of its young to fight for the freedom of even small nations and then had its very military return from those nations back to the U.S.? Just as Mother's Day was originally established in the United States as a day to reflect and remember those mothers who were no longer with us, I will never allow a Memorial Day to go by without sharing with others thoughts of those who sacrificed, even their lives, for the safe passage of America.

Recently, while appearing in a foreign country, I heard "The Star-Spangled Banner" played before a sports event. Once again, my heart and spirit swelled with pride. How fortunate I have been to enjoy my success here at home in the U.S.A. Irving Berlin was right when he wrote "God Bless America." God has.

Ray Ferry

THE AMAZING KRESKIN
World's foremost mentalist

Only in America could a little girl of humble beginnings in a small town in South Dakota enjoy a wonderful career in the entertainment industry, meet and marry a man of humble beginnings from Scotland, and see him sworn in as a proud American citizen. Through the grace of birthplace and the gift of choice, the American Dream has come true for us. God Bless America.

In an effort to give a little back to our country, in December 2001 we spent Christmas serving hundreds of meals to our troops in Saudi Arabia and Bahrain. The outpouring of gratitude from these extraordinary young people was overwhelming, but *we* received the greatest gift.

CHERYL LADD & BRIAN RUSSELL
Actor and producer

I consider myself **a quintessential American story.** My parents were brought to America through Ellis Island. They were poor but worked hard. My father went to work as a teenager in the silk mills in Paterson, New Jersey, as did many other European immigrants. He worked in the textile factories, helped harvest vegetables on a farm, and with a deep degree of embarrassment and humility worked as a laborer for the WPA—whatever it took to support his family.

After graduation from high school, I joined the Army and served in Europe during World War II. Afterwards, I was able to go to college—Columbia—with the extraordinary help of the GI Bill.

The government's "investment" in me seems to have paid a good return: after college, two friends from my neighborhood and I started a company, ADP. Today it employs over 40,000 people around the world.

After 30 years of building a highly successful company, I decided to give something back to this country that has been so good to me, so I became involved in public service—first as Commissioner on the Port Authority of New York and New Jersey, and then as a United States Senator, now in my fourth term.

America is a place where hard work is rewarded. It's also a place where the government gives a helping hand to those who need it. We need to make sure that America remains that way.

FRANK R. LAUTENBERG
U.S. Senator, New Jersey

I can honestly say that America doesn't suck!!! We are all so lucky to have such a free lifestyle. My hat comes off to the many men and women who serve and protect our U.S.A. so that we can enjoy this liberty. I've traveled the world many times over and seen just about everything. Trust me when I say these words...

TOMMY LEE
Rocker

America ROCKS!

In 1940, my family and I opened a single storefront selling dairy products in Cincinnati, Ohio. Our first day of sales amounted to $8.28. Today, our related companies provide insurance and financial services across the U.S.A. A favorite quote of mine is "Only in America," which acknowledges the opportunities afforded us by this great country.

CARL LINDNER
Chief Executive Officer, Cincinnati Reds

It seems to me that in America it's common for someone's life to be transformed by the pure force of a dream backed by preparation and relentless determination. I've been blessed with the opportunity to make a living playing the game I love, while people everywhere I go are fulfilling their own dreams as teachers, doctors, entrepreneurs–anything they want to be. Here in America people really can raise their families in peace and know that there is a bright future out there if they reach for it.

PEYTON MANNING
Quarterback, Indianapolis Colts

JACKIE MASON
Comedian

RAOUL FELDER
Attorney

Growing up as children of streets peopled by immigrants—no child having a parent born in this country—we had no real sense of connection with any community larger than our own neighborhood, yet even at that, there were no discordant elements. We all shared in the abundance of poverty that nature, or some mysterious force, bestowed upon us. But America was to our parents a refuge, a kind of Rubicon one crossed to gain entrance into a safe harbor, and, once there, life began anew with all the rights that should be natural to man—well, perhaps not *all* rights. There were hotels that would not accept you, and clubs you could not join and jobs you could not get, but you did not have to fear the midnight knock on your door or punishment for what you might say, or be required to have an identity card ... and if you were ov twenty-one, you could vote. America was, above all else to us, safety—a land surrounded by unfordable oceans that insulated us from evil.

Two or three wars later, all of this has changed. The barriers of exclusion and prejudice have been broken down, and if there was any question after the outrage of September 11th, anyone living in New York understood we were one country. There were police cars from Ohio, Pennsylvania, Delaware, and Texas, and firefighters from Illinois, Michigan, and a dozen other states, and all the varied accents and intonation of this broad land were heard across the city, and no one asked the race, religion, or economic status of th people who were buried or of the ones doing the digging. Today we are tailors and carpenters and doctors and scoundrels and cooks and architects and every occupation and race and country of origin and languag imaginable under the sun. There is no American "gene." Every person who ever came here, whether in the hold of a ship or in a first-class cabin of an ocean liner or on an airplane or crawling across a border,

remained here for one reason—the prospect of a better life. This common thread binds us together. This commonality, this chord, at once both real and almost mystical, joins us and in times of crisis is apparent for all the world to see and, if need be, relied upon. We are a celebration of what the individual, man and woman—free people—who allowed to chart their own destinies, can achieve. We are also a demonstration of the power of freedom itself.

Sadly, there are still among us those who have neither the courage nor the intellect to understand the burden that this freest of all countries has put upon its citizens. There are demonstrations across the country against the war in Iraq, and yet those who march do so in arrogance and with indifference to the fact that people in Iraq do not share a similar privilege. The marchers do not understand that freedom is not a virus that spreads to other countries by itself, but rather, it is a blessing we have and which we have a moral imperative to share. History will not allow us to put gates around our country. The world has moved together with a velocity previously unimagined, and it becomes a simple proposition: Evil in one place will be evil everywhere, and liberty bears with it the burden to be shared.

The reason I am proud to live and play football for a living is simple. Everyone in this country has the opportunity to do and be somebody, whatever and whoever.

DEUCE McALLISTER
Running Back, New Orleans Saints

We were three kids who grew up in New York City and got the chance to travel around the world as Run-DMC. We experienced many cultures and many laws and ways of living. After traveling to many countries and nations, we knew that it was good to be in America, the land of the free, free to be who and what you wanna be. We had freedom of speech and expression, and we were free to worship as we please.

Touching down on American soil, we knew it was good to be home.

DARRYL "DMC" McDANIELS
Run-DMC

America is simultaneously the most loved, hated, feared, and admired country in the world.

In short ... we're Frank Sinatra.

DENNIS MILLER

Comedian

I love this country because we have the freedom here to be what we want, go where we want, and say what we believe. Even though we have our share of problems, we're still the best country in the world. I love the U.S.A.! America has given me the opportunity to chase and reach my childhood dream to play in the NFL.

RANDY MOSS
Wide Receiver, Minnesota Vikings

I'm proud and pleased to live in the U.S.A., because it IS the greatest country in the world! It's truly a land of choice above all others.

As citizens, we have so many freedoms and blessings that so few other countries provide.

I'm forever grateful to the men and women of our military and their families for their dedication and sacrifices to help keep this great land and the world at large free from tyranny. God bless them, and God bless America.

MARIE OSMOND
Entertainer

I am a Sioux and Apache Native American, a German Jew born of an African slave. My mom actually picked cotton in the deep South and sat in on restaurants for integration with Martin Luther King, Jr., thus allowing me to be born in a country without Jim Crow standing on my back. We've come a long way as a nation, we've fought hard together and even against each other to create an America that belongs to us and generations to come. And like all strong families, it's all right if I attack you sometimes but nobody better not, never. I am America. Proud, strong, and free.

PAULA JAI PARKER
Actor

The American Spirit encircles our every action, protects our rights, and fuels our dreams. It continues to grant freedom to those not living it, and protecting those experiencing it.

Back in 1960, my family arrived in America fleeing from the grasps of tyranny and censorship. From that day on, the community embraced and provided them with opportunity that they needed to progress.

Forty-three years later, as Mayor of Miami-Dade County, I continue to return their gift, with a steadfast commitment to prosperity for all. That is the America that as sons and daughters, we continue to fight, dream, and defend all that it stands for.

We live in a great country, where responsibility to protect its freedom is but the greatest of rights for every citizen alike, and service, one of freedom's grandest privileges.

God bless America, her spirit, and all her glory.

ALEX PENELAS
Mayor, Miami-Dade County, Florida

The word "American" is the epitome of the word freedom.

It represents personal liberty, true sacrifice, and endless opportunity.

Being an American is to wake up in the morning knowing that I can strive to be the man I want to be.

CHAD PENNINGTON
Quarterback, New York Jets

When our nation's Founders signed the Declaration of Independence, they pledged their lives, their fortunes, and their sacred honor. They were deadly serious in making that pledge. When they picked up the quill pen to place their names on that document, they did so with the certain knowledge that it could cost them their lives, and many of them paid the full measure of their pledge.

The Founders believed in the people. They knew in their hearts and souls that each generation would have to work hard to pass on a greater nation to the next generation.

Nothing has changed. America's strength is its people.

We are deeply patriotic, creative, and dedicated. We are filled with love for our country. We are brimming with ideas. We are determined to leave something better for our children.

A Norman Rockwell painting, "Breaking Home Ties," shows a farmer and his teenage son sitting on the running board of an old pickup truck. The farmer, whose face and hands are wrinkled and gnarled from years of working in the sun, is wearing blue denim work clothes. His son is wearing a suit. They are waiting alongside a railroad at a whistle stop to flag down a train. His son is going to college. The father has worked and sacrificed so that his son can achieve the dream his father could never realize.

It is that determination, demonstrated by the love, character, and work ethic of my parents, that enabled me—a child of the Depression—to achieve the full measure of my potential. The basic lessons of honesty, integrity, and hard work, which my

parents taught me as a child, are the same lessons I have strived to pass along to my children and grandchildren. I am confident that they will help build a better nation.

My grandfather died when my father was fourteen years old. My dad had to leave high school to take care of his mother, sister, and younger brother. He later sent his younger brother to college. Throughout his life, my father helped people in need, although he had limited financial resources. My father is a classic example of a person who spent his life working to pass on a better country to the next generation.

It is this simple desire—to pass to the next generation a nation that is better than the one we inherited—that makes the United States of America a nation of good, kind, and decent people.

ROSS PEROT
Chairman, Perot Systems Corporation

I love the U.S.A. because of the freedoms we enjoy. The freedom to pursue our dreams … like enjoying and playing our national treasure, baseball. I've been blessed to pursue my dream of playing and managing Major League Baseball. It is a game that has always mirrored our country, and I am so fortunate to have spent a good part of my life in it. Every day I put on the uniform, every time I hear the national anthem before the game starts, I am reminded of those freedoms that we all enjoy. None of us, especially those of us in Major League Baseball, should ever forget it.

LOU PINIELLA
Manager, Tampa Bay Devil Rays

First of all, when I think of America, I think of a beautiful country. That's why a lot of people around the world like coming to America.

You see a lot of different ethnic groups because of the freedom. You get a freedom of expression, and you get to do what you want within reason. America represents freedom and equality for all, and with everything that is going on I'm proud to be an American.

PEERLESS PRICE
Wide Receiver, Atlanta Falcons

One day you're the little victim of bigotry, the next you're flying to London to meet one of the Beatles. That's my life and, baby, it's a journey that could have happened only here in America.

Back in the 1960s, while enjoying recess in my parochial uniform across the street from St. Leo's, a neighborhood bully charged up to me, spat in my face, shouted "Goddamn Catholics!" and fled. He was the same color and about the same age as me. I was a third-grader. My abuser had been taught that prejudice. He didn't know me. He had been fed the mental image that all Catholics were the same, that all Catholics were bad. That image was wrong.

I started my broadcast career on Milwaukee television as a film critic. I got my share of anonymous racial hate mail and nasty messages left on my voice mail after hours. Like the little boy in grade school, bigots hit and ran. Without an agent, I got myself a job with a local Manhattan TV station in 1985. Three years later and still without an agent, I had my own prime-time celebrity talk show on VH1. I loved that job.

During those wonderful years, I interviewed Paul McCartney in London. He told me that director Franco Zeffirelli offered him the lead in his 1968 version of *Romeo and Juliet*. I knew that film.

We saw it on a field trip when I was in high school. Exposure to the arts way back in Watts served me well on assignment in the United Kingdom.

I have heard numerous times from producers, casting reps, and agents that I was "too smart" or "not black enough" to get some of the work I wanted. Each one of the guys who said that was so white he was almost invisible. They had the wrong image of how all black men should look, act, sound, move, dress, and what they should know. The image was wrong. To imply that intelligence was not a hip, masculine, marketable ethnic quality hurt more than when I was spat upon.

It hurt me, but it didn't stop me. Professionally, my pursuit of happiness as my declaration of independence is something of which I am proud. My career has not always been a happy one, but, as Americans, we are not guaranteed happiness but the pursuit of it. Say what you will, that alone is a liberty not known the world over.

BOBBY RIVERS
Television personality

What is the American Dream? While we may each have our own specific goals, I believe the answer is found in the extraordinary combination of our differences. As a melting pot of diversity, our origins matter less than our destination, and our destination matters less than our journey. The true triumph of humanity is our overriding belief in the capabilities of the human spirit and our enduring struggle to protect the freedom we enjoy. As Americans, we are free to choose our own identity and free to live life on our own terms. Our country was built by people with great dreams and courage to take great risks.

It's a tragedy of the human spirit that so many people in the world can only imagine a place like America. Despite our ever-changing challenges, there is a pervasive spirit of courage and determination that is strengthened, not tempered, by our capacity for compassion and faith. And yet we are human, capable of experiencing the full range of emotions from excruciating sorrow to extraordinary joy. It's in the defining moments, when we perceive insurmountable challenges, that we look into our souls for direction and often receive unexpected strength from the selfless contribution of others in our community. In this way, we learn that each of us can work to change events in our daily lives, and it is the total of all those acts that creates the history of our generation and the legacy for our children in decades to come. Isn't that really the American Dream?

ANTHONY ROBBINS
Author, Awaken the Giant Within *and* Unlimited Power

Michael Halsband

Living in America means having the freedom to express my point of view, the opportunity to be all that I can be, and to live simply so that others may live simply.

It is perhaps best expressed by those who don't enjoy the freedom that we as Americans have been given.

DANIEL RODRIGUEZ

Actor

Living in America enables me to have the freedom to be whoever I choose, to do whatever I want, and say whatever I want. Being an American is a blessing and a curse. While we have all these freedoms, we are contractually bound to the consequences of our rabble-rousing.

CHRISTY CARLSON ROMANO

Actor

It is impossible for me to enjoy the freedoms we have here in America without thinking about the millions of quiet heroes who are responsible for their preservation. I'm not talking about those you read of in the history books or celebrate in story and song. I'm talking about people like Walter Backal, my late stepfather, who proudly donned his Army uniform in World War II, served his nation overseas, and returned to work and raise a family, never talking about his exploits or bragging of his bravery.

There have been countless others like him—from the Revolution through Iraq—who did the same. It is a unique and wonderful nation that produces these quiet heroes who are so willing to defend a concept, to fight for an idea, to die so that those who follow can live in freedom.

We owe so much to these men and women, whatever our politics and no  matter how critical we may be of our government or its policies. These freedoms we continue to enjoy have not remained in place without a very high price having been paid. All of us who live in America should forever be aware of, and grateful to, those who have paid for it.

PAT SAJAK
Host, "Wheel of Fortune"

Freedom means opportunity—and I am incredibly proud as an American to have participated in and benefited from the incredible educational and economic opportunities this country has to offer. When I came to America, I became empowered by freedom and the ability to exercise my free will and make choices independently. I believe in the values of freedom, the democratic process, and our responsibility to offer a voice to those less fortunate.

ARNOLD SCHWARZENEGGER
Actor and Governor, California

One of my favorite movies, *Sunshine*, chronicles one hundred years in the lives of a Jewish family who emigrated from Russia to Hungary. Although the Sonnenscheins believed Hungary to be their promised land, those hundred years proved otherwise. They were subjected to the upheavals of a monarchy, socialism, Nazism, internal fascist states, several iterations of communism, and, throughout it all, the religious persecution they thought they left behind in Russia.

What the Sonnenschein family hoped for but never realized in Hungary is what my family found in America.

Like the Sonnenscheins, the dream of a better life led my great-grandparents to immigrate to America from Russia. To support their families, my grandparents took meager jobs—at various times working as a peddler, a poultry vendor, and a prizefighter. My parents grew up in the Depression, but through hard work and faith in the American Dream, they, too, persevered. My ancestors passed on that entrepreneurial spirit and passion to me, which led to economic and business success that none of them would have thought possible.

We have taken the dreamers from all over the world, myself included, and given them a home where their dreams can become reality.

JEFF SMULYAN
Chairman & CEO, Emmis Communications Corporation

Having come to this country when I was five years old (I was born in England after my parents escaped the Holocaust in which a good part of my family was murdered), living in America has always had a very special meaning for me since it was not a birthright, but truly a gift from God. Moreover, and because I've lived at literally every income level imaginable in this nation, I also know from personal experience that the American Dream is far more than a feel-good shibboleth we mindlessly employ on the Fourth of July; it's real, and I am lucky enough to have lived it.

So if I have a cause for concern today, it is that equal opportunity, which is what lies at the heart of the American Dream and makes it possible, may not be as readily accessible to current and future generations as it was to me. And that is why I regard it as a personal obligation, and the highest act of patriotism any of us can perform, to do whatever is necessary to ensure that equal opportunity not only survives, but is once again the touchstone of our society.

It is, after all, what makes America ... America.

JERRY SPRINGER
Television personality

The privilege of being an American was impressed upon me many years ago, through my youth, by family members and various other mentors. I have long believed living in America and the freedoms associated with that are simply privileges, not entitlements. We are all born with the hope of freedom and opportunity in some manner. Yet those ideals and beliefs are not as easily attained in many corners of the world.

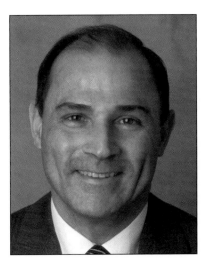

It is America that provides us an endless array of ever-changing liberties. It is America that allows us to disagree with our leadership and each other, while enabling us to do so without restrictions. And it is America that will continue to pave the way for the future of mankind through the spectrum of intelligence and development of knowledge.

But I am also reminded during the playing of the national anthem before each of our ball games, of the sacrifice, loyalty, and dedication of so many that allow us to enjoy and live freely in this great country.

BILL STONEMAN
Vice President & General Manager, Anaheim Angels

ISIAH THOMAS
NBA Hall of Famer

America is a place of great diversity, great challenges, and great change.

America provides the opportunity to become who and what you want to be through dreams and hard work. America is a place where my mother has laid the foundation for me and my family to live the American Dream.

America is my house. As with any house, there's always a lot to do, lots to enjoy, and things to change. Home is always a project.

 To me, America is a house of many varied chambers—geographies, histories, cultures and climates, architectures and cuisines—with a room for every fancy, every need. And, when we sometimes open a closet full of skeletons, it may be scary and painful, but we try our best to clean them out.

A house is brought to life by the people who live there, and we are a big, loud, busy family in America— neighbors and strangers included—all part of the project, believing, even in the midst of differences and debate, that America is a home worth working on, worth dreaming about, together.

RICHARD THOMAS
Actor

Phin Daly

We live in the greatest country this world has ever known. We live among the greatest heroes this world has ever seen, and we live with all the liberties of which one could ever dream. To be an American is to be proud, proud of the land we live in, proud of the people we are and the freedom to dream of the people that we may, someday, become.

BRAD ARNOLD
MATT ROBERTS
CHRIS HENDERSON
TODD HARRELL
3 Doors Down

To me. living in America means freedom. That is the first word that comes to my mind. As a businessman, that is closely followed by "equal opportunity"—which is also a form of freedom, and possibly the greatest form of liberty any citizen can know.

Do we know how lucky we all are to have a chance?

There are many countries where a very small portion of the population has the chance that every individual in this country is automatically granted. This is a wonderful gift—and an advantage that cannot be measured, except perhaps by those who have never had this kind of opportunity.

Words often fall short when we think of things that move us deeply, or that matter a great deal to us. That's how I feel about America. So I will have to end with the word that came first: Freedom. That says it all.

DONALD TRUMP
Chairman & President, The Trump Organization

America is not a dream, it is a reality.

Don't go against the impossible when the impossible wants to make everything possible for you. I love America.

JEAN-CLAUDE VAN DAMME
Actor

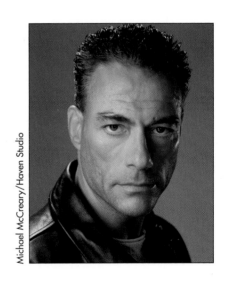

The Declaration of Independence states that our Creator deems us to have "...certain inalienable rights, that among these are life, liberty and the pursuit of happiness."

I take great pride in knowing that I live in a country that based its foundation on such noble and courageous principles. Courageous because our Founding Fathers had to foresee some of the hard work and sacrifices that would lie ahead of us. As citizens for the last 227 years, we have defended our homeland, protected our core ideals, and attempted to meet the challenges of living and prospering in a land filled with diverse races, cultures, and religions. The privileges we enjoy as Americans are afforded to our great country because we try, perhaps more than any other nation in the world, to work to overcome our obstacles.

After serving twenty-two years in the military, seventeen of which were active, I have seen a lot of changes. Changes in global policy, changes in race relations, and changes in mankind as a whole. Some people are still working toward defining what America's freedom means to them, while others continue to struggle with the inequities that challenge our nation. Even though we still have hurdles to overcome, the spectacular thing about our country is that regardless of whether we have achieved the success that we desire—spiritually, financially, personally, or professionally—the opportunity is available to each of us. I am proud to have served to protect those freedoms at home and abroad.

MONTEL WILLIAMS
Television personality

Living in America ... it struck me in the faces of 9/11.
For days running I reported on America's supreme tragedy.
Interviewing survivors and witnesses of Ground Zero was
to peer into portraits of grief and bravery. Such sorrow.
Such resilience. I was moved and humbled by the shock.

Crossing the threshold into 9/11's human experience was to
comprehend what America meant as reflected in the faces
of those lives changed because of her. In tearing us apart,
9/11 united our bonds as Americans. I felt enormous
pride in my country's strength—in hearing the tales,
holding the hands, seeing the faces.

PAULA ZAHN
News anchor, CNN

Andrew Eccles/CNN

I believe that the U.S.A. is a great country. I am proud to be an American, and I am thankful that all of us who live here have the freedom and the potential to accomplish our goals and to live the life our hearts desire.

JACKLYN ZEMAN
Actor